REALITY
TV
TITANS

SIMPLE SOLUTIONS WITH

Rachael Ray

Jill C. Wheeler

Checkerboard
Library

An Imprint of Abdo Publishing
abdopublishing.com

abdopublishing.com

Published by Abdo Publishing, a division of ABDO, PO Box 398166, Minneapolis, Minnesota 55439.
Copyright © 2016 by Abdo Consulting Group, Inc. International copyrights reserved in all countries.
No part of this book may be reproduced in any form without written permission from the publisher.
Checkerboard Library™ is a trademark and logo of Abdo Publishing.

Printed in the United States of America, North Mankato, Minnesota

062015
092015

THIS BOOK CONTAINS
RECYCLED MATERIALS

Design: Jen Schoeller, Mighty Media, Inc.
Production: Mighty Media, Inc.
Series Editor: Liz Salzmann
Cover Photos: AP Images, front cover, back cover
Interior Photos: Alamy, p. 25; AP Images, pp. 11, 13, 14, 15, 17, 19, 21, 23, 29; Corbis, p. 7; Mighty
Media, Inc., p. 27; Seth Poppel/Yearbook Library, p. 9; Shutterstock, pp. 3, 5, 10; US Department of
Agriculture, p. 22

Library of Congress Cataloging-in-Publication Data

Wheeler, Jill C., 1964-
  Simple solutions with Rachael Ray / Jill C. Wheeler.
     pages cm. -- (Reality TV titans)
  Includes index.
  ISBN 978-1-62403-820-4
1. Ray, Rachael--Juvenile literature. 2. Cooks--United States--Biography--Juvenile literature. I. Title.
  TX649.R29W45 2016
  641.5092--dc23
  [B]

                    2015009319

CONTENTS

Rachael Ray

Rachael Ray is among today's most popular celebrity cooks. Her fans appreciate her warm, down-to-earth style. Ray understands what normal people like to eat and how they like to cook. She believes food does not have to be **complicated** to be tasty.

Ray says she is not a chef. She has never taken a cooking class. Her success has come in part because she cooks the way many average people cook. This makes it easy for many people to relate to her.

Ray's friends often comment on her almost endless supply of energy. She is involved in many things, from television shows to magazines to cookbooks. She has written more than 12 best-selling books. She has created her own line of cookware. She also runs a nonprofit foundation focused on the issue of hunger in America.

RACHAEL RAY
2, 4, 6, 8
GREAT MEALS FOR
COUPLES OR CROWDS

food

Rachael
Ray with one
of her many
cookbooks

Food Family

Rachael Domenica Ray was born on August 25, 1968, in Glens Falls, New York. She is the second of James Ray and Elsa Scuderi's three children. She has an older sister, Maria, and a younger brother, Manny. When Rachael was young, her family moved to Cape Cod, Massachusetts. Her parents owned a chain of restaurants there called The Carvery.

When Rachael was still a young child, her family moved again, to Lake George, New York. A few years later, her parents divorced. Rachael's mother took a job managing a chain of restaurants. Rachael, Maria, and Manny often went to the restaurants with their mother. Rachael and her **siblings** always had after-school and summer jobs. They washed dishes, cleared tables, and sometimes helped cook.

Rachael was exposed to many cooking **techniques** while she was growing up. Her earliest memory is of watching her mother cook. Her Italian grandfather influenced her early experiences with food. He passed a love of Mediterranean style cooking on to his granddaughter.

Rachael's family says her first word was *vino*. That's the Italian word for wine!

City Adventures

Rachael went to Lake George High School, where she was a cheerleader. While in high school, Rachael started her own business creating and selling gift baskets. She called it Delicious Liaisons. At the same time, she continued to work in restaurants with her mother and **siblings**.

After graduating in 1986, Ray went to Pace University in Westchester, New York. She studied literature and communications. However, she left college after two years. She felt she needed to think more about what she wanted to do.

Ray got a job as candy-counter manager at Macy's department store in New York City. Soon she moved to the fresh foods department. When she left Macy's, she became a buyer and manager at the **gourmet** food store Agata & Valentina.

DID YOU KNOW?
When the cheerleaders made a human pyramid, Rachael was usually on top.

Ray *(center)* during her sophomore year in high school

Ray loved her job at Agata. However, the work was demanding and she worked long hours. After two years, she decided it was time to leave New York City. She headed back home to Lake George.

A New Direction

Back home in Lake George, Ray rented a small lakeside cabin. She took a job managing Mr. Brown's Pub in the nearby five-star Sagamore Hotel. Eventually, Ray found a job as a buyer at another **gourmet** food store, Cowan & Lobel. This allowed her to really see what customers were and were not buying.

Ray noticed that few customers bought the food ingredients she was selling. Instead, they bought premade meals. Ray wanted to encourage people to buy ingredients and cook with them.

The Sagamore Hotel is located in the beautiful Adirondack Mountains.

She started offering in-store cooking classes. They focused on meals that used simple ingredients and were fast and easy to make. Ray's classes were very popular.

Ray enjoys showing people how to make basic, tasty meals.

30-Minute Miracle

Ray's classes caught the attention of an Albany, New York, television station. They asked her to host a weekly **segment** on their evening news program. For each segment, Ray went to someone's home or workplace. She taught the people there how to cook a fast and simple meal.

By 1999, Ray had created enough quick and easy meal recipes to fill a cookbook. She called her first cookbook *30-Minute Meals*. She sold it in local grocery stores. The book sold an amazing 10,000 copies in just two weeks.

Two years later, a producer from NBC's *Today* show called Ray. He asked her to fill in for a chef who could not make a scheduled appearance on the show. It was snowing heavily, but Ray and her mother drove to New York City. Due to the storm, a drive that would normally take four hours took nine. But Ray and her mom made it to the studio in time. Ray did a segment on cooking soup. It was a hit!

Ray has published more than 20 cookbooks!

Winning Fans

Shortly after Ray's appearance on *Today*, the Food Network called her. They wanted her to do a program on the network. Ray didn't want to at first. She did not think she would fit in with the network's celebrity chefs. The network offered her a contract anyway.

Ray began working on two shows on the Food Network. The first was *30 Minute Meals*. In it, Ray continued to show at-home cooks how to quickly prepare fresh, homemade meals. The second program was *$40 a Day*. Ray visited various cities. She challenged herself to eat three restaurant meals a day for less than $40. Her viewers

Ray returned to *Today* in 2005. She shared Thanksgiving cooking tips with Al Roker.

learned the secrets of locating good, inexpensive restaurants where locals eat.

Viewers found Ray's programs to be a welcome change of pace from other cooking shows. Unlike many chefs, Ray used boxed or canned ingredients. Sometimes she clattered pans or dropped things. But instead of filming the **segment** again, Ray would keep going and make a joke about it!

Onward and Upward

By 2002, both *30 Minute Meals* and *$40 a Day* were hits. The Food Network rewarded Ray with more programs. In 2004, she began hosting *Inside Dish*. On that program, Ray visited celebrities in their kitchens. The following year, *Rachael Ray's Tasty Travels* **premiered**. In this show, Ray traveled the world trying different kinds of foods.

At the same time, Ray continued to write best-selling cookbooks. She expanded her 30-minute meals idea with 30-minute comfort food recipes and **vegetarian** meals. Then came 30-minute meals for entertaining, as well as cooking with kids.

In 2001, Ray attended a friend's birthday party. There, she met a lawyer and musician named John Cusimano. Ray and Cusimano ended up talking for hours. Afterwards, they saw each other or talked on the phone every day. They got married in Italy in September 2005.

DID YOU KNOW?
Ray went on to create seven successful cookbooks featuring 30-minute meals.

Ray with her husband, John Cusimano. He is in the rock band The Cringe.

Magazine Founder

Her marriage wasn't Ray's only new venture in 2005. That year she launched *Every Day with Rachael Ray*. The **lifestyle** magazine features cooking tips, shopping advice, and recipes. It also has articles related to home decorating, travel, and pets.

The first issue came out in November. In 2006, there were six issues. Soon publication increased to ten issues per year. As editorial director, Ray sets the direction for the magazine. She also opens each issue with "Rach's Notebook." In it, she introduces the issue and **highlights** the main topics.

Every Day with Rachael Ray received recognition almost immediately. It earned Launch of the Year honors from both *Advertising Age* and *Advertising Week* magazines.

DID YOU KNOW?
Ray's magazine's cover usually has an image of Ray or a dish featured in that issue.

EVERYDAY

WITH RACHAEL RAY

74 *foolproof* **Recipes**

LL WITH PHOTOS!

LAX!
tress-free
holidays

AST & EASY
0-MINUTE
MEALS

ET OUTTA TOWN!

truly
asty

68 COOL GIFT IDEAS

The first issue of Ray's magazine

Talk-Show Host

In 2006, Ray started her own talk show. From the first **episode**, *Rachael Ray* was very popular. And it has won three Daytime Emmy Awards. It received one for "Technical Direction/Electronic Camera/Video Control" in 2007. It won for "Outstanding Talk Show/Entertainment" in 2008 and 2009. More than 1,500 people have been guests on *Rachael Ray*. They include singer Miley Cyrus, athlete Derek Jeter, and First Lady Michelle Obama.

Entertainment insiders say Ray's likable personality has helped her show succeed. *Newsweek* called Ray "the most down-to-earth TV star on the planet." *People* magazine gave the show a top-ten ranking for 2006.

The praise is no surprise for Ray's fans. They love her **trademark** sayings, such as calling extra virgin olive oil "EVOO." And they appreciate Ray's recipes and time-saving tips.

DID YOU KNOW?
In 2011, Ray guest-starred on the TV show *30 Rock*.

Ray on the set of *Rachael Ray*

Stardom led to roles for Ray outside the kitchen. She was on *Dancing with the Stars* in 2006. She has been a guest on *The Tonight Show*, *The View*, and other talk shows. Perhaps the biggest sign of Ray's success came in 2007. That year "EVOO" was added to the *Oxford American College Dictionary*.

Hunger Awareness

One of Ray's common phrases is "yum-o." She says the word just came out of her mouth one day when she combined "yum" and another phrase beginning with "oh my." The term stuck.

In 2006, Ray started a nonprofit organization called Yum-o! The organization helps kids and their families develop healthier eating and cooking habits. It gives kids and families tools to cook easy, affordable meals at home.

Through Yum-o!, Ray created a special school lunch recipe for schools in Chicago, Illinois.

The group's website includes information about cooking and feeding the hungry. Yum-o! also works to help provide **scholarships** to young people who want to work in the food industry.

Ray and Senator Kirsten Gillibrand talk to children in Washington, DC, about nutrition.

In 2011, Ray worked with the American Association of Retired Persons. They **collaborated** on the Drive to End Hunger. It was a public service campaign to help older Americans with hunger issues.

DID YOU KNOW?
Ray's favorite color, orange, is also the international color of hunger awareness.

Animal Advocate

Ray loves animals, especially dogs. In 2008, Ray created Rachael Ray Nutrish. It is a line of dog and cat foods and treats. Ray uses some of the profits from sales of Nutrish foods to help at-risk animals. The money is divided between a number of animal shelters and rescue organizations.

Ray also partnered with the American Society for the Prevention of Cruelty to Animals (ASPCA). Together, they created the ASPCA Rachael Ray $100K Challenge. It challenged animal shelters to work harder to save more animals. The shelter that saved the most animal lives each year won a grand prize of $100,000. The challenge ran for five years, from 2010 to 2014.

In 2014, Ray **donated** more than 174,000 meals to KittyKind. KittyKind runs Meow Parlour. It is a café and cat shelter in New York City. There, customers can eat snacks while visiting the cats. Many choose a cat to adopt!

Ray at a charity event for the Animal Rescue Fund of the Hamptons

Life Today

Today, Ray is very busy. She creates about 600 new recipes every year. She often has four or five jobs at a time. Sometimes she does not get home until ten o'clock at night. However, she still loves to come home and cook. Ray now owns the Lake George cabin she first rented. She and her husband also have a home in Southampton, New York, and one in New York City.

In her limited spare time, Ray enjoys watching cop shows on television. She also goes to hear her husband's rock band, The Cringe, perform. And most days she runs several miles for exercise.

Ray refers to her success as a happy accident. She always knew she wanted to work with food. But she didn't imagine things would turn out as well as they did. Ray's fans often thank her for helping them be less afraid of cooking. "Then I know I've done my job," Ray says when she hears this.

DID YOU KNOW?
Ray has a pit bull named Isaboo.

Inspired by Rachael Ray

Broccoli Mac 'n' Cheese

Serves 8

Ingredients

- **16 ounces elbow macaroni**
- **16 ounces broccoli florets**
- **salt**
- **1 tablespoon olive oil**
- **2 tablespoons butter**
- **½ cup chopped onion**
- **1 cup ricotta cheese**
- **½ cup shredded Parmesan cheese**
- **black pepper**

1. Ask an adult for help.

2. Cook the macaroni according to the directions on the package. Drain it and set it aside.

3. Put the broccoli in a pot. Add just enough water to cover it. Add ¼ teaspoon salt. Bring the water to a boil. Cook the broccoli for five minutes. Drain the broccoli.

4. Put the oil and butter in a deep frying pan over medium-high heat. When the butter melts, add the onions. Stir and cook for 7 minutes.

5. Turn the heat to low. Add the broccoli and macaroni. Stir them together.

6. Stir in the cheeses. Add a little salt and pepper.

Timeline

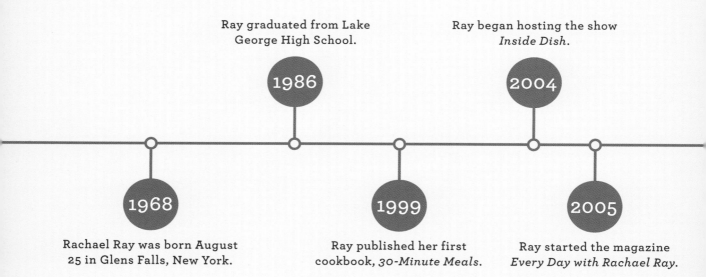

Ray graduated from Lake George High School.

1986

Ray began hosting the show *Inside Dish*.

2004

1968

Rachael Ray was born August 25 in Glens Falls, New York.

1999

Ray published her first cookbook, *30-Minute Meals*.

2005

Ray started the magazine *Every Day with Rachael Ray*.

Rachael Ray Says

"My life has been a total accident—a very happy, wonderful accident that I didn't and couldn't have planned."

"Decide what it is that you are and then stay true to that thing."

"How good is that?"

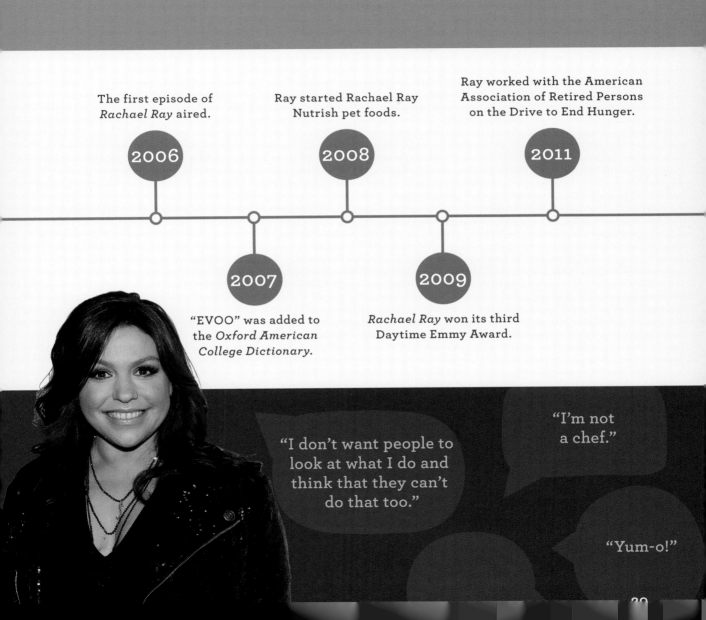

The first episode of
Rachael Ray aired.

2006

Ray started Rachael Ray
Nutrish pet foods.

2008

Ray worked with the American
Association of Retired Persons
on the Drive to End Hunger.

2011

2007

"EVOO" was added to
the *Oxford American
College Dictionary*.

2009

Rachael Ray won its third
Daytime Emmy Award.

"I don't want people to
look at what I do and
think that they can't
do that too."

"I'm not
a chef."

"Yum-o!"

Glossary

collaborate – to work with another person or group in order to do something or reach a goal.

complicated – having elaborately combined parts.

donate – to give.

episode – one show in a television series.

gourmet – related to fancy or expensive food and drink.

highlight – to point out an important or interesting part of something.

lifestyle – the way of a person, group, or society lives.

macaroni – a type of pasta in the form of small, curved tubes.

premier – to have a first performance or exhibition.

scholarship – money or aid given to help a student continue his or her studies.

segment – a scene on a specific topic that is part of a news show.

sibling – a brother or a sister.

technique (tehk-NEEK) – a method or style in which something is done.

trademark – something, such as a way of dressing or speaking, that is typical of a certain person.

vegetarian – not including any meat, poultry, or fish.

Websites

To learn more about Reality TV Titans, visit **booklinks.abdopublishing.com**. These links are routinely monitored and updated to provide the most current information available.

Index

PEACHTREE CITY

PLAN TO STAY™

PEACHTREE CITY LIBRARY
201 Willowbend Road
Peachtree City, GA 30269-1623
Phone: 770-631-2520
Fax: 770-631-2522